Weasel in the
Turkey Pen

Other books by Marie Harris:

Raw Honey (Alice James Books)
Interstate (Slow Loris Press)

(Co-editor, with Kathleen Aguero):
  A Gift of Tongues: Critical Challenges in Contemporary American Poetry (University of Georgia Press)

  An Ear to the Ground: An Anthology of Contemporary American Poetry (University of Georgia Press)

(Editor): *Dear Winter: Poems for the Solstice* (Northwoods Press)

Weasel in the Turkey Pen

by Marie Harris

HANGING LOOSE PRESS
Brooklyn, New York

Published by Hanging Loose Press
231 Wyckoff Street
Brooklyn, New York 11217

First Edition
Printed in the United States of America

Hanging Loose Press thanks the Literature Program of the New York State Council on the Arts and the Fund for Poetry for funding in support of the publication of this book.

Acknowledgments: *Paragraph, Hanging Loose, Sojourner, Z Miscellaneous, Penumbra, Rural Heritage, Bluefish, Poetry Now, Longhouse, Breakthrough, Red Brick Review, Stray Dog, Heaven Bone,* and *Keltic Fringe.*

Special thanks from the author to Jean Pedrick and the poets of Skimmilk Farm for their constancy, criticism, imagination and support. And to Marjorie Fletcher for shaping these poems into a book.

Cover design and photographs by Charter Weeks

Library of Congress Cataloging-in-Publication Data

Harris, Marie.
    Weasel in the turkey pen / by Marie Harris. — 1st ed.
        p.   cm.
    ISBN 0-914610-80-5 (hard cover) :
    ISBN 0-914610-76-7 (pbk.) :
        I. Title.
    PS3558.A6475W4   1992
    811'.54—dc20   92-18015
                                                    CIP

 Produced at The Print Center., Inc., 225 Varick St., New York, NY 10014, a non-profit facility for literary and arts-related publications. (212) 206-8465

CONTENTS

I

II

III

IV

for Charter, again

I

AIRBORNE

In the racetrack parking lot, just a few spaces down from "The Tent: where brotherhood is more than just a word!" where Christian bikers (beautiful bellies, glowing tattoos, vests embroidered with "Riding for the Son") man a table of free apples, homemade chocolate chip cookies and hand-lettered pamphlets about Jesus, a group of clean-cut young men are filling helium balloons one by one to make a single enormous balloon which is being tied to the bound wrists of a naked inflated woman-doll with a hank of synthetic yellow on her head, legs spread at a cartoon angle and orifices that are painted a stunning pink. She seems to be saying "O!" in wonder and anticipation as the boys fill the last balloon and pull her into the open where the crowd in the stands, alerted, turns as one man, astounded into clapping and laughter while the inflated woman tugs at her tether, spins, rises above the hot, gleaming bikes, moves into cooler air, ascending more rapidly now into a blue background pillowed with clouds. They cut the string! She banks over Turn #8 and heads out. Her heart is pounding so loudly that she cannot hear the applause or the whistles or the screaming engines.

DIVINER

She walks at a measured pace, her eyes focused at a point just beyond the fork of the hazel stick which she holds lightly at shoulder level. Veins of clear, potable water tremble under the skin of the earth. She follows to where they converge. Her hands tighten; the waters pull the stick down until her wrists bend backward. "Here," she says and says how deep. Lately, she has been called upon with terrible frequency, for it is also true that she can find the severed limbs of women beside an interstate, wives with bruises on their faces, fathers who have betrayed daughters, videotapers of kidnapped children, wilding boys. At these times her stick abrades her palms, breaks into blossom like Joseph's rod.

TORTURE

Her mouth was held open by a recent invention called the rubber dam. It felt obscene. It made her gag. Moments earlier, her pleasant dentist had administered electric shocks to each front tooth. She was to indicate, with a motion of her hand or a gargled cry, if they were still alive. She had lied about the second tooth, claiming to have felt the electricity even though she hadn't. Now, as she waited through the drilling and filling, as her neck muscles contracted and her palms grew moist, her thoughts bounced back and forth between the twinges in her own nerves and the pain she knew was right then being inflicted on women in cells, in basements, in clean, brightly lit rooms. The mind, she thought, is a terrible thing. Released into an afternoon of insufferable heat, she drove out of town and was stopped by a cop for a routine violation. He loomed at her window, enjoying her discomfort. Only a job description stood between him and the man he wanted to be. She lost her temper and yelled at him, half her face twisted in anger.

STANDARD PLUMBING

Plumbing supply places, like auto parts stores, have long counters with bar stools for the customers. When I came in, the man behind the counter was telling a story about the time he and his friends had decided to celebrate getting home from Vietnam and had bought a lot of Scotch and given one bottle to a wino who drank half of it all at once and dropped dead. Then the man, with *Walter* stitched on his shirt, asked what he could do for me and I told him I had come to buy a toilet, the cheapest, most basic toilet they had. He wanted to know if I was putting it in one of my apartments or something and I said no, it was for my own house and I was, oddly enough, buying a toilet for the first time because we were installing indoor plumbing. The other houses I'd lived in had always come with toilets and I'd never given much thought to choosing one, though today I'd kind of decided I wanted bone, not white. So, in the process of getting the bowl and the tank and the seat and some pipes and gaskets from the warehouse, we got to talking about our outhouses and he allowed as how the one he had in Florida when he was a kid in the fifties hadn't been all that bad, except for the bugs and sometimes a snake, and we both agreed that there are times out there when you see things from an unusual vantage, for instance: that view of the night sky in winter is unparalleled.

THE SEVENTH DAY

Up the road from the Town Dump, this side of the ballfield, the sand pit is an arena defined by snow fence sagging in the heat where neighbors made strangers by a long winter drink beer, wait for the annual horse pull to begin. Today there will be no clearing of pine stands, no emptying fields of rock, no hauling of hay. Today, as if in deference to the commandment, paired and harnessed in Sunday leather and brass, they will pull and pull a stone boat to no practical end. Two men will gallop behind them with the hitch. One man will drive them. He will shout like a preacher *Back! Back! Back!* until they become at a crucial instant one gathered muscle, one heart, one astounding, weightless lunge. And they could pull, on a fulcrum of hoof, the weight of the world.

WALKING ON ICE

Léonard jabs a pole into the ice in front of him as he walks, hatless, into the wind. He is followed by a knot of camera-hung tourists delivered in helicopters to his old hunting ground. Blue-green scabs on the skin of the sea. Drifts. Pans, cracked through with watery leads, deep black. Blood on the ice. Afterbirth of harp seals that followed underwater maps to the floes, dropped their glittering, big-eyed mewing pups. Time was Léonard and his neighbors loaded heavy wooden *canotes* with weapons and gear, dragged and floated them out miles over frozen terrain for the season's meager cull. Whitecoat pelts and sweet seal meat. Blood stained floating March ice for centuries. Blood brought protesters like gulls. SAVE THE SEALS. Now the hunters are hungry and the seals are saved, fat wilderness exhibits, well photographed. Wind stitches all the cries. Léonard pokes the slushy ice, picks a safe path, answers the eager questions of strangers in orange survival suits.

MAKAH CULTURAL &
RESEARCH CENTER

Mud slid over the coastal village of Ozette like dawn, halting each life on a man's inhale, his sleeping shift from belly to back, the child's nightmare and the woman's restless stirring. Mud filled the cedar rain hats and boiling baskets. It stilled the spinning tops and harpoons and swift sea canoes. Old arguments went unresolved, suspicions unconfirmed. *"This,"* said Mud, *"is everything you are now. Treaties and lies will conspire to erase your future. Lie down. Trust me."*

THE FIFTH DAY

By this time there was light and dark. The waters were gathered and separate from the firmament. Dry land bloomed. Birds inhabited the skies and the oceans swarmed. There was one morning, abrupt and brilliant, a long sigh of a day exhaling into gray evening, and one night full of starry krill. On this the fifth day the whales composed all their songs as they broke the skin of the sea with their black backs and drank from the cold broth, sounding and surfacing, fluke and brushy plume. Their choruses recall, even now, the hours before dominion.

GOLD

A rain competes with the glowing afternoon in one of those speeding microclimates in which something unusual is bound to happen. And it does. Suddenly she sees a segment of rainbow and pulls the car to the edge of a sliver of shoulder on a road in northern Vermont alongside a rattling brown cornfield. The end of the rainbow has landed smack on top of a small white frame house at the back of the field. She wants to tear through the corn, bang on the door, tell the occupants that they have just this instant hit the jackpot. But before she can move, the rest of the rainbow appears, its other end planted in the opposite corner of the cornfield. Beneath the apparition, she is as transfixed as Lucia at Fatima. She gazes at the celestial stripes in their luminous entirety for two, maybe three minutes. Then the whole rainbow disappears in a gust of gray cloud and the rain diminishes to drizzle, to mist.

TENT CIRCUS

The cop clown is out back sitting on a hitch, nursing his sciatica while the Puerto Rican balancer shares a ring with his juggling son. Jana is changing out of her jungle queen cat tamer outfit into her trapeze rig. She still hasn't got the neck spins right. The ringmaster announces himself, then eats fire. Tonight the old man with the dancing poodles fills in for the chimp trainer who has allergies. Nostalgia hangs in the multicolored air. Lumbering behind their aging aunties, the last baby African elephants in captivity turn circles. They roll on their backs for the shrieking children. They remember nothing. They are post-modern elephants, the final orphans.

THE STARTER: LEE, USA

He stands on the balls of his feet, tense and ready in the cold white light, in his box at the point above the track where it banks steeply and falls toward the starting line. He is magnificent in white light: bright blue short-sleeved shirt tucked into the waistband of bright white crisp pants, tan hand passing mechanically through bright white hair. The race you watch will be his race at every turn so, when the Modified Streets have come onto the track, after the drivers finish swerving back and forth in tight patterns to test the steering, test for error, once they settle into the paired positions they have won, watch the starter. Watch him.

He focuses his attention on the flashing school of cars. At his back, an ovation of flags, each in its stand, snapping in the summer evening wind. Their moves are for the eye; you cannot hear them above the speedway noise, but will imagine the sound from flags you have heard before. His assistant hands him two, furled. The yellow. The green. He bounces the poles lightly in his hands as the fishtailing racers gun their engines. You do not need to pay close attention until you see him hold the yellow-and-green in parallel out from his body as if in benediction. Then he begins moving them in tandem, up and down. All things being as equal as they are at this moment, the race will start on the next lap. Watch.

He is watching the Streets. Now! He looks up at his flag. The green flag. He looks at the way he spins it. Twirls it. Makes it do figure eights against the black sky in the bright white light. Pulls it out of the sky right down to the ground. And now! Only now can they break as he leaps and lands with the green flag cutting down. He twists his whole body to follow the start, spectator for that moment.

Keep watching him above the distraction of the speeding cars and you will understand everything.

Look! He is waving the yellow flag furiously. Furiously. Furiously. Something dangerous. The race stops in motion. He puts the flag in a sleeve. It flutters over the track. He turns away, lights a cigarette. Nothing of consequence will happen without him. Sometimes the spun car returns. Sometimes it pulls off into the pit. The yellow flag remains until the field is correct. Until he matches yellow with green, furled. Again. Do you see the pattern?

He has more. White. Checkered. Red. The combinations! The possibilities! He could hold crossed flags aloft...now...and the race would be half over. He could signal two laps to go with a white-and-checkered, or create the finish with the checkered. Better still: checkered and yellow: a win and a danger together.

Or he could turn his back, light another cigarette, leave his platform and walk toward the silent parking lot as his racers chase shadows, held in their positions—winner and losers—by his abandoned flag.

THE REASON FOR SPORTS ON TV

for Bill & Sebastian

Someone won the British Open today. In basketball season I
watched the Lakers or the Pistons or the Celtics playing, play-
ing off, because in some room, three hours earlier than time
here, my sons were probably sprawled on a Salvation Army
couch watching the playoffs, the plays, their leg muscles
twitching in empathy. This afternoon in a bar, the overhead set
is green with golf, the commentator reciting its hushed liturgy.
The players are older, comforting, almost, in their restraint.
They are alone with their game. It used to be, if I wanted to
spend time with my father, I would watch a match with him:
in silence, rarely venturing a comment on the game he himself
played so well. He would speak of the golfers in tones he usu-
ally reserved for the President and men of the cloth. He
became expansive in the presence of golf; between strokes he
was able to talk about other things openly, even to a woman.

FIELD GUIDE FOR THE END
OF A CENTURY

A young voice surfaces at unpredictable intervals on my answering machine as though this boy had become trapped within it. He vents his pent-up rage on the tape. He knows my name, of course; I introduce myself to anyone who calls. The more polite my message, the more obscene his. Yesterday he screamed, his voice cracking, along three intervals, becoming more furious each time his time ran out. Sometimes when I garden, as I pull somber red rhubarb stalks from the plant, I wonder how many tries it took for man to sort out the properties: the tingling possibilities of the lower stems, the poison in the leaves.

S. DALI IN MONTRÉAL

Dali speaks into a receiver that contains the lobster's sweetest meat. He hears the wind as it must sound even today in corners of Auschwitz. He pulls open one of the drawers that he's built into Venus de Milo, only to discover the bra of Venus which he himself did not fashion. Dali has calculated in color the speed at which Raphael's Madonna will explode into its component parts. He putters in reflections and histories: Hitler's mustache as landscape by moonlight, desert topologies, elephant swans, her. Dali cannot bring Gala back. Not in oil or glass or pencil or bronze or mirror or gouache or clay or clock. His attempts, though, crowd the last room of the exhibit.

ARTIFACTS

In the country the Indians called The Backbone it is huckleberry time, a time of foraging bears and fat elk, of sudden snows in the mountains, morning fog in the valleys. Bighorn sheep and mountain goats graze in precipitous pastures, appearing and disappearing like shadows on the rocks. The road to the skeleton of the St. Eugene Mission threads a pass pocked and scabbed by loggers.

Until the arrival of white European pioneers, Indians had lived throughout the far reaches of the Kootenay for thousands of years....Priests of the Oblate of Mary Immaculate imposed completely new social and political structures on the converted.

I approach the school down a driveway lined with trees that look foreign in this piney, bony landscape. Neither cedar nor lodgepole, these are Catholic trees.

The convent school of childhood forbade entry to certain rooms. Now a mimeographed Self Guide ushers me to a priest's lounge, the sleeping quarters of the sisters, their bathrooms. At the end of a first floor corridor I come to a confessional made of plywood, a peeling plaster holy water font, the chapel.

An Indian woman greets me. "I was a student here for eleven years." Her eyes are cast down as if from unbreakable habit. "Now this is our museum." I follow her past a hand-drawn map showing the ancient sprawl of her people along the rivers. "Kootenay. It means water."

Many of their artifacts have survived to this day, including the distinctive Kootenay canoe, superb white buckskin clothing and finely fashioned stone tools.

Old glass cases, half empty as if they had been looted, hold meager relics: a piece of lead ore, faceted arrowheads, a *parfleche* and little pair of faded moccasins, dried roots and seeds. At the altar end of the room stands a white tipi and a dog travois. Draped on a hanger there's a white garment, fringed and beaded from neck to hem, and beside it a feathered lance.

The Kootenay region has a rich cultural heritage whose protection and interpretation to future generations is vitally important.

The walls of the chapel are pallid and cracked, the floor scuffed by the hard soles of vanished communicants. I have a question for my guide, but she has disappeared. I can stay no longer.

Driving away past winking towns, past car dealerships named after Indian tribes, I stop for gas and buy a cheap key-chain in the shape of an arrowhead that says "Kootenay Country" in elaborate script. I attach it to my keys as if it were a St. Christopher medal. Down the road, a nighthawk hurtles against my windshield and falls, wasted, on the dark highway.

TAMMY BAKKER'S LEFT EYELASH

Like Burma Shave ads in sepia photographs, dozens of signs stick in the dirt beside Route 15 on the way to the ferry to Prince Edward Island. ANDY'S DUMMIES JUST AHEAD. Hand-lettered in red paint. ANDY'S DUMMIES WILL MAKE YOU LAUGH. Then a beached dory overflowing with bosomy creatures, their Clorox bottle heads tipped and touching, at the entrance to a driveway under a big sign. ANDY'S DUMMY FARM. FUN FOR ALL. And Andy himself, a gnome with a neat white beard, plaid pants, doctor's smock, a clipboard, all prepared—genial spider in the center of acres of wooded web—for the bemused tourist who will follow him down piney paths peopled with his stocking-stuffed politicians and drunks and evangelists and happily blowsy women, each hung with placards, pronouncements on cigarette smoking, acid rain, politics, sex, religion. Indestructible detritus hangs from tree limbs. Pie plates. Bottle caps. Blue laundry baskets. Plastic doilies. TAMMY BAKKER'S LEFT EYELASH. Tucked amongst wildflowers, floating in rickety dories on a scummy pond, leaning on barns and outhouses, generations of dummies, some faded to the colors of the forest, some as bright as mall mannequins. WE ALL LIVE IN A YELLOW SUBMARINE YELLOW SUBMARINE. A woman drives up, stares for a moment, slams the car into reverse. Still time to catch the boat to the land of Anne of Green Gables.

TOURIST HOME,
PRINCE EDWARD ISLAND

Mrs. Brown's visitors come in the wrong door and must be brought through her kitchen and living room past Mr. Brown who sits silent on the sofa cradling a wrist which is bound up in a cast. All the furniture is covered with brown and orange crochet work. Mrs. Brown brings the couple up a steep flight of stairs to their room. A fall coat and a red pocketbook hang on a hook outside the door. The three jockey for position between the iron bed and the bureau. A breeze lifts a corner of the patterned plastic curtain, bringing the scent of wild thyme and cut grass. There are inspirational pamphlets on the bedside table and a collection of hankies in a Japanese box on the dresser. "You can leave the door open for the air," she says cheerfully. "It's just our two families." The bed is noisy. It sags into a trough in the middle and the couple sleep fitfully. In the night one of them goes into the bathroom. Caught in the dull yellow of a nightlight: paper badges stuck to the wall opposite the shallow tub. HELLO, says each one, MY NAME IS Nina Brown Stanley Brown Nina Brown Nina Brown Stanley Brown Nina.

THE BEDROOM

The bed has a chronic list. The side on which no one sleeps is strewn with empty envelopes and among them notepapers, pink overdue notices, stained appointment cards dating back months, church newsletters. Near the telephone with its tortured cord is a coverless phone book and two gaping handbags. At the foot of the bed, a yellowing girdle, twisted pairs of pantyhose, a neat stack of blouses with their yard sale tags hanging from tiny gold safety pins. One hospital-issue foam slipper. A housecoat. A plastic cosmetic case with a broken zipper spilling capless lipsticks, stale powder, dulled eyebrow pencils.

The bedside table is littered with brown bottles labeled with her name and the names of doctors. Some are dusty. Some are empty. A few are stuck on daubs of congealed cleansing cream. Scattered like a broken string of beads: her caplets and tablets and spansules and gelcaps.

On the vanity under a windowsill full of withered plants, there are combs choked with orange hairs, pocket mirrors, balls of cotton, iridescent scraps of butterscotch cellophane, instructions from a box of ear stopples, the label off an oxygen canister.

"Come in, dear. Make yourself at home."

BELAFONTE IN BEVERLY

Harry, son, his tiny Jamaican mother admonished him, *never sing a song you don't like because that's sure to be the one you'll have to sing for the rest of your life.* But there he was again, crooning "Yellow Bird" to hundreds of grandmothers-in-the-round. They loved Harry. Yes, he was fit as they remembered, and still so handsome. When Harry sang "Matilda" they sang along. When Harry sang Mandela and starvation and freedom they tapped their feet. They could even imagine Harry living next door. *That's him*, they'd say to their sleepy husbands at dawn, *it's Harry. DAY-O!* His island voice confuses the robins and chickadees. *DAY-AY-AY-O!* He's standing on his front porch in flannel pants and tassel loafers; his tight gray curls glisten with dew as he calls into the suburban morning while he absently strokes the tarantula in his palm. *DAYLIGHT COME AND ME WANNA GO HOME.*

II

ZUMBADOR

The words we choose to learn will determine the nature of our experience. How much? *¿Quánta cuesta?* Where is? *¿Dónde está?* May we object, *por favor,* to those aspects of your culture that make us uncomfortable? We are only here for a short time, so we would like you to pay special attention. *¡Camarero!* Food. Food is very important to us. *Tengamos hambre.* Now and then we would like *tipicas.* We are trying to notice everything. Our phrase book, *¡aye!,* has no word for hummingbird.

LUQUILLO

This is a town not far from the airport in the shadow of a mountain rainforest in whose depths flitters the suggestion of rare parrots. Birds we may never have heard gather in trees we do not recognize. Tiny lizards decorate the walls. Does one kill them? A woman laughs abruptly and steps back into a court-yard.

SAN GERMÁN

The uninvited perch on low walls like pigeons; they gossip, they speculate. Newly wed, bride & groom pause on the top step: behind them orange sun & lime white church. Her girl-friends & *tias & primas* pluck at each other's shimmering cloths while the men smoke & smooth their hair, smooth pants. Below in the courtyard, members of the Sabana Grande Motorcycle Club rev the engines of the Harleys that glisten like pomaded hair. This is the moment. She lifts her ruffles & begins the descent. The guests school, washing her and the thin boy at her side down into the gathering noise, the revving. The sound is almost visible. The bikers mount. Turn on lights. Gun engines. They carry the couple off past townspeople on wrought iron balconies, past tourists surprised in their new rooms, past the ones behind turquoise shutters. What follows is the story.

AMONG STRANGERS

The hotel pool is within a courtyard open to the sky. Overhead, a section of wooden church tower with clay pots for bells shows above the tiled roofs. I discover that the manager is lately arrived; he and his wife and son have for many years lived on a boat. The man is very, very busy. It is clear by the way he moves that he enjoys his work. The boy is big for his age, loud, rude, smart and obviously lonely. He bashes a beach ball from one end of the pool to the other while his mother tends to her nails or writes in a notebook. She sits at a white table all day, several rows from the pool's edge. At night she is joined by the man and the boy. They are served their dinner amongst the guests. Between courses the boy jumps into the pool.

If you approach her she will tell you many things about her life and the lives of her parents. And though her story is set in another country, you will recognize familiar features on the landscape. She is restless. Intelligent. Even ambitious. She shapes and files the edges carefully. She uncrosses her brown legs in a gesture that might be your own. I am tempted to befriend her, but she detests her life so thoroughly, in such precise detail, that instead I recoil, as if in fear.

PONCE

Dónde está a *restaurante* that serves real food *pero* fast food is what's happening in Ponce & fast country-western blaring from speakers on the tops of small trucks & the whole town's in the streets. *La iglesia* is worth a stop *y el museo, pero* the parking is impossible and it's so hot you won't want to do anything or even stay very long.

LA GALLERA

It's the men wedged together on peeling bleachers in rings above the circling cocks. It's the noise of shouting men over the spectacle of two glistening birds, one white one black, flying at each other, beak and spur, neck feathers in a fan of blood-stained rage. It's the fingers of men, thrusting money signals across the arena. It's the smell of men: perfumes of beer and hair and sweat. It's the armpits of men, cradling their birds; and the hands, stroking a wing, holding an ice cube gently on a swollen eye. The cocks battle. The men watch all day with sharp eyes. Then they go out.

MOCA

They know where to tell you to find her—straight ahead, *toda derecha*—because she's always been there, spider woman, rattling her polished bamboo sticks, weaving filaments. I step out of the white afternoon into her tiny cool world with its brown light. She springs alive when she sees me, races back and forth among the shelves and glass cabinets. "*¡Mira*, lady! Look!" She pulls delicate collars and tiny booties onto the counter, unwinds long lace trim. Everything is spread before me. Her grandson scoots past and disappears through a curtain. (Where are the women to sit at her side, teaching their fingers to knot flowers?) I hesitate, unable to choose a single delicacy from the foamy piles. She feels it, like the tremble of a fly on silk. "*¡Mira*, lady!" She scuttles behind a windowed case, opens a little door, snatches a plaque from its place next to the Virgin of Guadeloupe. "*¡Bar-bar-a Boosh!*" she shouts exultantly. And there it is: a laminated thank-you note, bordered in presidential blue, proof that this work is beautiful.

WHAT YOU CAN EXPECT TO SEE OUT THE CAR WINDOW BETWEEN ENSENADA AND MAYAGÜEZ

In every town: bright yellow buildings, beauty parlor & barbershop signs painted on the walls, *REBAJAS*—shoes, children's dresses, cameras, men's shirts—ON SALE, tiny hairless dogs, storefront Christian churches that open at night.

Along every road: little white egrets and the cattle they ride, white truck with four flats and an awning of thatch (pineapple, coconut, Malta in cans), fields of *piña*, fields of cane, fields of glittering salt edged by fragile stilt houses, glimpses of the sea, of mountains.

And everywhere: plastic cups lids rings labels tabs bottles spoons trays straws.

MANNY IN RINCÓN

Manny changes into salsa colors an item at a time: pair of flip flops, mirror sunglasses and a hat—a Panama-style hat with a hatband. First thing you know our boy looks right at home, looks great in hot pink, looks around at the place we tell him he was born and he likes it, yeah, nice place. And when they speak to him in Spanish he smiles and nods. Nice sounds, never mind he's nodding at the drunk in the bar who's asking him if his mother wants to dance. He drinks a *piña colada sin ron* and gets a little older, looks right. At home he looks all wrong. Wrong colors. No place for turquoise. But here it's the sky and the shutters, the sea and the store sign. Yeah. Nice.

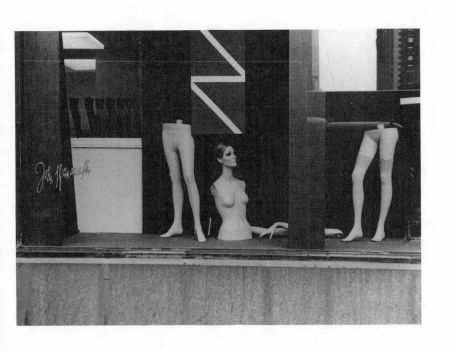

III

WEASEL IN THE TURKEY PEN

It's one of the mysteries of nature: arguments begin late at night. They don't, of course, begin as arguments, but as discussions over a beer or glass of wine between two reasonable people who share similar attitudes. They have spent another day in each other's company, working at all the tasks that fill a day, and the last chore left undone as the whip-poor-will begins its monotonous beat and mosquitoes whine in gathering crescendo, is to close the turkey chicks into the coop.

The night deepens to cricket buzz and low wind. It's the perfect time for talk. Their conversation lengthens. They have discovered several points of disagreement and are talking louder. One of them has stopped listening. One of them repeats an assertion, rephrases it for emphasis. One grows exasperated and notes it's very late. The woods outside are silent as bats, suggesting presences. This would be the perfect time to sleep in familiar embrace and let dreams untie the knots they've made. But they pass across that time.

In the morning the evidence is so plain, so mundane. The little turkeys are all in the pen; only the heads have disappeared.

MARY CASSATT AT THE DINER

Years ago, when she was young and her children very young (she might have been their older sister), she had agreed to meet her husband's anxious student-lover in a back booth and had stayed for the duration of her babysitter's hour (though half of it would have been enough) to hear an earnest exposition on the reasons for her husband's dissatisfaction, his need to bed more attentive women, the necessity of his having a real wife, a wife without professional ambition, in order that his objective correlative life might teem with the sensory stimuli so crucial to his art. It made a certain amount of sense, looked at from that viewpoint, dispassionately. Sipping tepid, pale tea from a thick white cup, the saucer of which rested near a glass vase of roadside chicory, she thought of the wives of the Impressionists.

TRIAL SEPARATION

I rented a little windblown house with two bedrooms and a single tree in the back yard onto which every morning evening grosbeaks descended like a brief squall. I bought new sleeping bags and a green record player for my sons. I changed my brand of dish liquid to one that smelled exactly like fresh peaches and found a part time job reading the papers of a freshman science fiction class. I invited a younger man to dinner. One afternoon a painter came by and admitted he had always loved me. A visiting poet and her lover spent an evening in my bathtub. My friends told me I looked wonderful. By late spring my husband took to calling at odd hours to talk about himself and ask me to come home. It was time, he said. I packed up, drove the eight miles to a house where, in my absence, the kitchen had been painted too yellow and his study was a cold shade of blue. When I turned down our bed I found a red stain on the sheet.

GAME

He himself was a kind of terrier, all bristly and unkempt about the muzzle. Gameness was a trait he valued above all others; he bemoaned the lack of it among the general populace. This was a world, he often remarked sadly, filled with golden retrievers. Soon after we met, he painted my portrait. The sitting made me feel beautiful for the first time since the divorce. I wore a dress made of old, thin, black velvet that I'd found in a yard sale. I posed for hours in his drafty studio while he held forth on how you had to attack the canvas like a terrier—never afraid of it, never quitting—and the whole time he was slashing at his easel, pacing, backing up, slashing. The finished portrait was spare and elegant. He painted me often, though as time went on I became a less than willing model. As a result there exist, in closets or on the walls of friends and dentists, scores of renderings of a woman reading, her face in shadow.

He had drawbacks as a lifelong companion. He did not believe that artists should be distracted by domestic chores or gainful employment. His laundry piled up; I washed my own clothes. One day I let fly at him with all the ripening tomatoes on the kitchen windowsills. Another time I demolished a chair. After we parted he continued to like that in me, the gameness.

FIRES

Sunday. Brothers and sisters in pyjamas in the bedroom watching Disney. Dad goes to the connecting bathroom, sees smoke seeping under the door. *Fire!* He shouts. *Fire!* Then a tumble of older children and babies down the staircase. We pile into the Plymouth station wagon and wait, as if for midnight commuters. The upstairs windows are pink. Our parents are somewhere in there when the firemen come. Our mother helps them unfurl a hose. Our father is powerless to stop the flames. In the end, the whole house burns from the inside out. We go to school in our cousins' clothes, heroes.

The father of this brawling brood rakes leaves at night. In the morning, he leaves for work, flips lighted matches into his neat piles. The fire department arrives in the afternoon while he is gone. My mother makes coffee and charming excuses.

A Monday or Tuesday night. The alarm sounds. My husband has to excuse himself from a faculty cocktail party to be with the children while I, the volunteer fireman, speed in my own car to the blaze. Tonight it is what I will later call the Great Union Springs Broom Factory Fire. Timbers sizzle into the snow. In my oversized boots I drag heavy hoses off the truck. The women make coffee.

The fires persist. Brush fires. House fires. Car fires. I leave two sons and a borrowed daughter behind, where they will be safe, if not happy. Now I must save myself. I will return someday to claim them. Their clothes will fit them poorly, will reek of smoke, but we will have survived, the fire fighters.

THE END

We talked as though we were strangers, side by side on the
deck of a boat near Jeffrey's Ledge on a summer Sunday; but
the subject was familiar. We pulled in flashy mackerel, apricot
squid, tossed them back. We hauled up dogfish; we caught the
same ones over and over. They were heavy as waterlogged
boots. And stubborn. Gaff. Pliers. Knife. It was a struggle.
Finally I showed him what to do. *Pin it with your foot. Grab the
snout and break it backwards. Dump the dogfish overboard. Watch.* It
spun like a wild compass needle, thrashed in sinking circles.

DRIVING DRUNK

A station on the radio plays jazz, the kind that gives a beat to the zipping dotted lines, keeps time with the blurred bridge struts, truck stop signs, faraway towns jittering light. We're heading home and happy. My body is a reflex, part of the mysterious workings of an automobile. The windows are rolled down. The wind carries smells of fog and salt and fried food. Music oils the pavement and the car holds the turn as I downshift off the highway onto a small dark road. My husband runs his hand along my leg. *We'll get there,* he says without words. *Stay near the speed limit and pay attention.* Jazz, night, another humming journey home. Unbidden, moments from my past present themselves like a show of shuffled slides, out of sequence, discrete. One old transparency comes into focus like a distant headlight in the rear view mirror: it's the middle of an ordinary day on a road that climbs above Cayuga Lake and I pull the car, noisy with sons, off to the shoulder. They wonder why. I tell them something that satisfies them: *A heron is lifting over the water!* or, *Look at the sailboats!* But the reason I can't continue is that their father is sleeping with many other women and I feel like driving this car into the next phone pole.

CIVIL DEFENSE

My name is shouted from the steamy woods. I hide from it, stumble back into the cave of half-sleep. *Marie!* and again my name: *Marie! Bring the gun!* Now I hear the chickens wailing. Now I can make you out, all naked, white limbs among black pines, shining a thin light up into the tangled dark. *The gun!* Still stumbling. Downstairs. Which gun? I take the shotgun from the wall. What threatens us? *Here, dammit, hold the light. You brought the wrong shells.* I hold along the line you point and wait, covered in mosquitoes. *Can you see it?* No, I can't see it, can't see anything without my glasses.

> Once you had to shoot an injured squirrel. The
> blast blew the little animal across the snow; birch
> bark hung in tatters where it had been. The sound
> of a shotgun is nothing like Bang Bang.

This is only a test. Soon I will climb back into sleep, my fears subsiding like the muttering chickens. If this had been an actual emergency (I've thought it through carefully) we would shoot first the dog, then the housecats...

PEACETIME

You were four days sailing in gale force winds and ten foot seas: the impossibility of eating a meal or sleeping for more than a couple of hours before being thrust awake by wild pitching or the insistent shove of huge following seas; the necessity of steeling leg muscles against the constant shifting of the boat. You told me you'd been really scared. An intelligent response, I thought, to danger. You told me that the skipper said, more than once, "Thank God we didn't bring the women!"

Months ago, floating lost in Tasbapauni's inky lagoon, both of us had flinched under the orange tracer bullets. You confided later that you'd planned to cover my body with yours. I, on the other hand, was thinking only of myself. I would dive out of the *panga* and swim underwater where bullets are slow. Is that what the skipper meant?

SWIM

Mars floats upside down in the midnight pond as though the lacquered sky, tipped by our angle of vision, let slide that one planet while the stars depend on the stems of their constellations. Our moon-white bodies disturb the surface, intrude random longings into the peculiar logic of night: silence deepened by frog continuo; darkness unchallenged by cold stars; utter stillness limned by a looping, diving bat.

BIPLANE

So here we are in goggles and white silk scarves. We have reached the point of no return, the square of sky labeled DO NOT TURN BACK. NOT ENOUGH FUEL. There's nowhere to go but into the clouds, streaked and purpled with sunset. We look at each other, but cannot speak above the din of wind and propeller. We smile bravely, two movie stars in an impossible plot. Night comes. The wings begin to ice up. The engine misses a beat. The instruments are on the fritz. You know the story...with a few variations, it's an old one, but it still has power to make you hold your breath or clutch someone's hand in the dark. (Will they make it? Can they hold out until dawn? Will the cloud cover tear for an instant, revealing a plowed field, a deserted beach, some rough landing place?) You need to believe in us.

KILLING TIME

The pig's pen shrinks around her. The wattled turkeys are overblown: white chrysanthemums. A bluejay strops its call on a leathery wind. The simplest vowels clot in my throat. I stare at the old hen's head on the stump. The eye milks over; the beak finishes its death sentence.

PHYSICS ONE

Each cord of wood that warms this house—ragged hickory, chalky birch, maple, oak rounds that hold a fire overnight, arthritic apple, biscuit wood—has been carried, hauled, cradled, thrown, turned, stacked, handled—from standing timber to ashes for the outhouse—eleven times. Figured this way, the cord weighs forty-four thousand pounds. May those who would split the atom to make their fires first feel the weight, the heat of one cord of wood.

DEEP WINTER

Even our voices have gone into hibernation. With the frog and the tulip bulb, we have accepted this purgatory of silence and darkness so complete it is almost impossible to imagine light sufficient to rouse the croak and bloom of another season.

"AND THEN THE WINDOWS FAILED"

In a sector of day that contained neither star nor bird, I was wakened by a fly. You were still beside me. I was overwhelmed by a grief that had no reassuring ritual. Still your breaths came even, undisturbed, as if to exhort me to count them slowly, one by one, stilling fear, quieting the gossipy mind. The fly buzzed. I gathered cloudy images and framed their blue-gray patterns in the windows above my bed. Like clouds, they took the shapes of people lost. *I will die,* you breathed, *and you will be sad.* Loss is the part I know.

VALENTINE

Familiar enemies have wiped out the flock of Barred Rocks, rooster and all, save one. She carries on, fussing about in shavings and snow, falling upon the ordinary kernel of cracked corn as if it were a prize grub. She putters all day, settles on the empty perch at dusk. Has she gone mad? Doesn't she realize she is alone in her chicken world? Is it possible that I would continue without you, mumble on, still hearing answering noises? That the weak sun would rise and set as usual on my busy days; that I might scarcely notice the silence, the cold?

PATIENT, FEBRUARY

The pale sun, inclining, touches the tops of the swamp maples.
This time of year I pay attention to small changes. I lean my
elbows on a *prie dieu* of light as though spring required an act
of faith. As the afternoon turns deeper orange, I rock, wait for a
call from someone who is decoding my blood, reading the
shadows in my chest. Stubborn as a twelve-year-old, I am sure
that my body has a half life of a hundred years. But at this
moment there is just the fading day. No spring. Not yet.

ACTUAL GRACE

The earth is beaten into dull stuff. A smudge of sun rides under the bellying sky. Winter is finishing slowly, like sap over a wood fire. At Phil's Restaurant, breakfast customers hash over the Town Report. We still have our say. We still sing our annual hymn of republic and objection. Now, while sugar steam drifts, like March weather, eastward, we lift our chalices of syrup to the resurrecting light.

IV

TABLEAUX

Our Lady of Fatima

Mary is a blue apparition in the grotto on stage. We are the only ones who see her: three children dressed in what the nuns imagine are peasant wools and headscarves. Interrogated by priest and parent, still we hold fast to our vision, will not deny her secret messages. She promised a sign. Stage left, the villagers mumble like thunder. Stage right, the heavens darken, the sun careens toward earth, spinning and growing huge. As Lucia, the eldest, I am given one line: *The sun! The sun! Look at the sun!*

Queen of the Angels

Mary is a whited statue in the convent garden. We are the handmaidens in white linen, singing at the top of our lungs: *O Mary we crown thee with blossoms today.* The procession breaks in a circle at her feet. I climb the ladder with my burden of lilacs. I crown her with blossoms. I have been the perfect girl.

Mater Admirabilis

I am lying on a hotel bed. Two brown chairs make stirrups. The doctor goes about his business, practiced as a priest at the weekday altar. There is a woman in the window across the street—a seamstress. I am very young and without skills.

WHITE

The photograph is browning but the frame still gleams: a baroque affair, dense with silver storks and songbirds nesting in silver marsh marigolds and roses; a tiny silver scale and a miniature clock with its hands stilled at ten past eight flank the engraved words: ARRIVED NOVEMBER 7, 1943 WEIGHT 7 LBS 14 OZ. The baby's fat chin nestles in the puckers and tucks of a fine, white chemise. She is smiling. This is an early portrait of me: the first daughter of the first daughter: Marie. I will have, as a baptismal gift or a spell from a guardian angel, a privileged and happy childhood.

I am posed in front of a white fence just before or just after the event. Not the layered First Communion dress nor the cuffed socks and shiny shoes, not the tulle veil fixed to my hair with elastic and bobby pins can draw attention from the scabbed knee or the healing scar above my upper lip. I am clutching a little white missal and a bunch of flowers. I can recite perfectly and in order every answer in the Baltimore Catechism.

I am confirmed in white with a red sash that symbolizes the blood of martyrs. I take the name of Saint Agnes, though I'd have preferred (for this is my time of zeal and romantic missionary fervor) to take the name of Maria Goretti who gave her life to preserve her virginity from a lustful, knife-wielding field hand.

And although, throughout my Convent schooling, I am daily dressed like some proletarian worker, forbidden make-up or bodily ornamentation, there are Feast Days and May Processions requiring a uniform white dress and veil. There are flowers and music and slow walks down aisles.

How natural, then, it must have been for me to mount the carpeted stairs of the Waldorf Astoria wearing a white taffeta gown, my neck set off by a scoop of tight pleats, my arms covered to the elbow in white kid gloves. At my wrist, a thick gold bracelet; at my waist, a white gardenia.

That's me smiling in a line of debutantes decorating the mezzanine like lilies. Our fathers stand groom-like behind us. Mothers and grandmothers whisper just outside the frame.

Our escorts arrive to take us from the fathers, lead us onto the vast ballroom floor. My two are tall. I am dancing with the dark one. Perhaps a foxtrot. Now I am dancing with the blond one. Now, in my father's arms, I am waltzing. It should have been wonderful.

The Cardinal appears in our midst. He loves us. One by one we crumple at his slippered feet, heads bowed to kiss his garnet ring.

Marie is wrapped like an elaborate gift in yards of off-white satin and antique lace. She is at the heart of every picture. Around her, linens and china, silver and glass, flowers and candles. The white guest book overflows with names. She knows the answers to new questions, smiles graciously in response to them. Finally, she is given to everyone like slices of dry, white cake.

VINTAGE

It is almost as though, when I am at my scintillating best, I must mar the occasion: red wine on white tablecloth. The first time this happened I was lunching with a tall, elegant Jesuit priest, a scholar and man of the world. He had invited me to talk with him; I was a student, daughter of one of his ardent families. There had been no pause in the conversation as the waiter applied linen napkins to the stain. At a hushed restaurant in a small French city, as I was on the verge of stunning my husband with the brilliant inevitability of our lives together, and before the cheese course, I sent a crystal glass of Fleurie spinning to the beige carpet. In the fluorescent mall, at a plastic table at Papa Gino's, twenty minutes before the movie, accompanied by my two teenagers, I tilted one, then another glass of screw-top Chianti onto the linoleum. I have spilled wine in Spain, Puerto Rico, Québec City, Prince Edward Island, Paris and Minneapolis. Once, at naptime in the Convent of the Sacred Heart near the drama closet, I stole among the velvet skirts and breeches and braided jackets, plucked at amber beads and pearls and purple buttons until they ran in rivulets across the bare floor like fine wine.

THANK YOU NOTE

Dear John G:

Granted, I'm a few years late, but it's been on my mind and remembering how crucial the note was to the smooth operation of the social system into which both of us were born, and because neither of us knows at this point whether either has escaped the worst results of all that note writing, i.e. that we might have turned into extraordinarily polite liars (though your steadfast politeness is what I think of now and something that, of course, I never appreciated when we were that age), and though it's been a long time since we stepped onto a polished dance floor (you in your patent leather pumps with the grosgrain bows, me in my strapless peach taffeta dress with dyed-to-match heels that made me just your height) and executed the most elegant foxtrot, rumba, waltz, tango, samba steps of any couple on any of the dance floors we ended up on (who knows why; we never even kissed that I recall), I want to tell you it was Wonderful. Marvelous.

MY LAST CONFESSION

was a romantic affair: Christmas, Paris, Notre Dame. Alone and dressed for the occasion in something Piaf might have worn, I poured out the whole story, from my point of view, in English; the good Father listened in French and forgave me everything. I absolved myself, and the last breath of prayer I would offer for the life I was leaving ascended like candle soot, adding another layer to the darkened Stations of the Cross.

ASSUMPTION

August 15, 1986

Years ago your mother, old and blind, donned her black bathing suit, took the blue-veined hand of the monsignor (himself in black to the knees) and they walked through dunegrass to the ocean.

Take your ills to the sea on this day and bathe them away.

The feast is upon us. You are ailing and far from the sea, but we could walk, hand in hand, through burdock and ironweed to the river. You would take your ills and float them, like so many regrets, downstream. We will not bring the black dog, for he would fetch them back.

LAKE BOATING ADVISORY

This is a fiberglass boat wandering among whitecaps blown like daisies by the wind in a random fashion. I am among friends, nothing at stake: not my reflexes nor the finish. But supposing it were the last leg of a race and I was in the bow of a wooden boat designed to fly on a windward tack like the lead Canada goose in an angry sky; and supposing this were my father's boat, and my hands raw on the sheet, and I needed my father to love me...

LO!

Rose Phillipine Duschesne was not young when she arrived in the New World from France with her vineslips and her suspicion of eating seafood. She was equally distressed by the color of the Mississippi and the "savages for whom we made this journey." The Indian children gave Blessed Phillipine a name: *The Woman Who Prays Always.*

You get what you pray for. For instance, when the novice finished her fresco of Mater Admirabilis, the colors were gaudy, hideous; she hung a cloth over the wall to hide her shame and retreated to pray. Next morning, when Mother Superior pulled the linen away, lo! the painting was perfect.

In school we were meant to kneel up straight, rear ends well away from the benches. We got "convent knees."

Short prayers, designed to be prayed anywhere, on the spur of the moment or in emergencies, are called ejaculations.

You pray to different saints depending on what you want. You can pray directly to Jesus, but if you petition the Blessed Mother to intercede, it works better.

Fiacre (AD 670) is the patron saint of gardeners. Gengulf (AD 760) is the patron saint of unhappy marriages. Francis de Sales (AD 1622) is the patron saint of writers. Joseph, Husband of Mary (1st c.) is the patron saint of death (happy). Andrew Avellino (AD 1608) is the patron saint of death (sudden).

One of my sisters knelt by her bed every night during her eleventh year, with her head in her clasped hands, praying for the death of our father.

CEREMONIES

*

Every day she wakes an instant before the baby stirs. She changes him, feeds him, sits him near Morning Pro Musica and a vase of fresh flowers while she makes coffee. Knowing what he cannot know, every morning she must watch over his dying.

*

The doctors consult their secular missals for chemical prayers. They send my hapless friends into sterile cubicles humming with soft hits. In the rooms the nurses come and go, talking of shoes and Giorgio.

*

We have gathered where the ashes can finally be buried in spring-soft ground. Relatives and old friends and grandchildren fidget politely in their fashions. The robed priest arrives at the tiny hole in the grass, breathless from High Mass, a noon christening on his mind. He hardly knew our father. He opens the book to the final chapter and reads his lines. Into the silence he leaves, a little granddaughter speaks. "Is that it?"

*

I hold this dusty bird, its whole body pumping out a life into my palm. I wish I were still very young so all I'd need was a candle stub, some dead insects, milk-soaked bread, a shoebox lined with kleenex, a friend to help dig.

DINNER AT LOCKE-OBER

My friend brought me to her favorite restaurant so we could talk in a quiet place, eat soft-shelled crab, drink the best wines. As it happened, I spent as much time with our talkative waiter as with her. She was, I realized later, furious.

But I am the daughter of the man who lies propped in a hospital bed with a green oxygen tube in his nostrils, breaths coming and going at unfamiliar intervals. Now and then his eyes flutter open, seeing no one. My mother is there with a thermos of mushroom soup, and a sister, and me. A sheet, strung like a shower curtain, separates us from a man in the adjacent bed who is sick but not terminal. The TV on its wall-mounted arm insists a game show on all of us in that temporary bedroom. At one point Mom turns to me with tears in her eyes. "I've never seen anyone die!" Before I can answer she has pulled herself together for the nurse with a blood pressure cuff, the visiting priest.

My dad was always easy with cops, tradesmen, the proprietor of Rip's Diner who fried 'bowties' on the grill, the 300 pound taxi driver, the mailman who had a nip and a chat in our kitchen every noontime, the guy who plowed us out in winter and worked the summer garden, the men who drank beers at the Taco House in the morning and, after Dad quit drinking, the girls who filled his special coffee mug every day when he stopped at the counter on his rounds.

I stayed by Dad's bed for hours. More sisters and brothers came. We cried with each other in the halls. Sometime during the watch a stranger in a camel coat walked into the room. Mom rose to greet him, arranging her face, trying to place him.

Dad opened his eyes and sat up, disconnecting the IV taped to the back of his hand. "Frank!" It was the last word he ever said.

MOTHER ON A NORTHERN BACKGROUND, WITH CHILDREN

Your husband is dead and our voices have multiplied, like Mickey's brooms in The Sorcerer's Apprentice, into a chorus of admonitions. Shop less! Adventure more! Act like us but act your age. Travel for hours in the back seat of Dad's old car while we drive to St. Jerôme where we will all pile into tiny rooms at a small motel and talk about your grandson's hockey prospects and the siblings who aren't here. Sit on cold benches with your mink tucked under you for a cushion. Follow the plays and cheer. If you insist, we'll take you to Montréal for lunch at the Ritz with your dressy college girlfriend. We'll accompany you to tea at the mountain home of your old Canadian beau, then compare you to his new wife and speculate amongst ourselves on the interesting possibilities that might have ensued. We'll urge you to stay up late with us on New Year's Eve, and ask you to find a Mass for yourself on the first-of-the-year Holy Day of Obligation. We don't do church anymore. We sleep late.

MIDSUMMER BLUES

for Annie

A summer later I drive that familiar combination of back-road and Interstate (July smell of hay down and green corn, greens in the hills and trees, midsummer blues in the sky-border between New Hampshire and Vermont), drive to our mother's house, thinking of us, sisters together, and what brought us back to her bedside, her sickbed, over our own corduroy roads of marriage-and-children.

It used to be you and me against them. I remember that time he made her cry over a missing button on his shirt. We did not speak to him for days, though he did everything to warm our hard little hearts.

If we had known then what we can only imagine now! We could have let him be the hero, her the lucky one. They would have been so happy together.

GENERATION

for Raven
6/10/92

A little boy fetched me a yellow and black caterpillar from the underside of a milkweed growing at the town dump and threw in a starter bunch of leaves. It got me thinking of my old little boys, and the windowsills of their childhood, as I prepared the Mason jar, the waxed paper lid, secured it with a rubber band and punched the holes.

Funny how the mind summons random memories. Funny how I chose that day to telephone one son and hear that he and Rochelle had started a child.

Daily, I replenished the jar with fresh leaves and watched for the spin of sea-green, gold-studded chrysalis into a black purse filled with folded monarch wings.

Their new boy has finally emerged onto the ledge of family. I was there to watch him stretch his curled limbs, tilt toward milk-white light.

Each of us turns in the dream of flying, of flight.